umbilical discord

‏اِيتِل‎

ETEL ADNAN
POETRY SERIES

Edited by
Hayan Charara and Fady Joudah

umbilical dis cord

rawand   mustafa

The University of
Arkansas Press
Fayetteville   2024

ISBN: 978-1-68226-263-4
eISBN: 978-1-61075-829-1

28 27 26 25 24   5 4 3 2 1

Manufactured in the United States of America

Designed by William Clift

♾ The paper used in this publication meets the minimum requirements of the American National Standard for Permanence of Paper for Printed Library Materials Z39.48-1984.

Cataloging-in-Publication Data on file at the Library of Congress.

contents

foreword

What is the work of the witness facing broken time, facing into histories disappeared? How does the project of removing evidence of a people's existence reverberate across generations, geographies, bodies, selves? How to be steadfast in speaking back and through such violence, and to know the steadfastness of those who came before? These are questions unloosed in Rawand Mustafa's *Umbilical Discord*, a poetic sequence that powerfully dwells with, and brings the reader to, the endurance of Palestinian women's stories across the many displacements and losses of ongoing Nakba. As a text, it both is and enacts an extraordinary work of ethical witnessing—and these many months into Israel's current genocidal onslaught on the people of Gaza, of the West Bank, of Palestine, the urgency of its witness could not be greater.

In *Umbilical Discord*, Mustafa composes a multivocal dialogue across time, encompassing her re/presentation and translation of women's stories of invasions and flight in 1948 and after, and of contemporary diasporic locations and subjects. Working from formal and informal archives, Mustafa crafts poems from, and intersecting with, translated excerpts of Palestinian women's narratives.[1] In five movements—"dis cord," "dis location," "dis section," "dis ease," and "re cord"—her book-length sequence encodes a multiplicity of overdetermined cuts and relations onto the space of the page. An at times pronounced, at times invisible, distance is written between the indented,

---

1. In her afterword, Mustafa describes "scouring" the online archive of Zochrot—"a nonprofit association based in Tel Aviv that seeks 'to broaden [within Israeli society] the recognition of the Nakba and the Palestinian refugees' right of return' "—for testimonials by Palestinian women.

italicized column composed from Mustafa's spare and lyric translations of narratives from the Zochrot archive and its left-justified companion—contrapuntal locus of the reading eye and reflexive consciousness of the diasporic Palestinian poet. Reckoning with and recording her own family histories and retracing the breaks in a scattered matriline, the writer's— and by extension, the reader's—desire and ethical implication are at stake. These are poems of yearning and of being, both in spite of and fractured by an impossible history. As Mustafa writes in "re cord":

what is it
that moved me
> *the first time*
> *I saw my sisters again*
> *was in '79*
> *when we went to* قبرص
to trace
this umbilical
re cord?
> *you don't want to know*
> *what happened*
> *when I saw them*
to shed my
ignorance
> *my elder sister*
> *came out of the car*
> *and I recognized her*
> *somebody else came out*
masked
> *and sat down next to me*
> *she said*
> *"how are you?"*
by innocence?

> *and she started kissing me*
> *I told her*
> *"first tell me*
>
> I dig through
> my Stories Archive
> *whose daughter are you?"*

Like the gaps breaching the words that title Mustafa's poems, which also pull together towards meaning, the distance between the two halves (or split temporalities) of these poems at times almost disappears. Mustafa's composition not only activates the shifting space of this gap to inscribe traumatic loss and colonial displacement across geographies and languages but also mediates haunting and violent repetitions, proximities of feeling and intuition, longing for *and* responsibility to one's kinship, people, and identity. A devastating and dissonant resonance exists between her family's flight from state violence in Syria and earlier exile from Palestine.

> *I wasn't born*
> *in* لفتا
>
> I stare at the ruins
> of Yarmouk
> *my memories*
>
> uninhabited streets
> bullet holes in cement
> missing chunks
> of wall and roof
> empty window frames
> *are what my mother and father*
> *used to tell me*

Even as the testimonial voices in the italicized, indented column shift from poem to poem (and some threads on this "side" of the poems are fashioned from the testimonies of several women), the left-justified column speaks in a voice that is both collective and singular. Singular in the sense that while it incorporates stories from parents, aunts and uncles, and cousins, it is also specific to Mustafa, the poet who listens, inherits, unearths, and composes poetic space for holding this multiplicity of voices across the temporal folds and breaks of the text and the multiple colonial histories that continue into this present moment.[2] She thus renders visible in a radical way the texture of specific familial herstories and locutions of Palestinian women's resistance—and the long duration of Zionist attempts to destroy both Palestinians as a people and their historical and living relation to the land.

> *they put people in trucks*
> *and sent them to Gaza*
>
> we leaned
> on the side of the boat
> *and after they*
> *deported people*
>
> the speed
> unfathomable
> *they sat*
> *in their place*
> *and told us to go*
> *to the mountain*
>
> and the ship

2. At the beginning of the book's fourth poem, "dis ease," the temporal line within the poem's columns is crossed and displaced as the poet introduces to the left-justified column a story she has translated from her aunt's Facebook page, which in the afterword she describes as a chronicle "of a dangerous sea voyage from Egypt to Europe with her family and other Syrian refugees."

still watching us
but from afar
>
> *"whoever we see tomorrow*
> *at eight in the morning*
> *we will slaughter"*

they likely realized
we were on our way
to perishment
>
> *civilians were running*
> *barefoot*
> *blood oozing*
> *from their feet*

so they did not
advance
>
> *we stayed*
> *in* اللقيه

I invoked the contrapuntal earlier, perhaps inevitably recalling Said's famous use of the musical term to figure a reading process attentive to the inscription of dominant (colonial) and submerged or marginal (colonized) narrative perspectives.[3] It functions otherwise here: in writerly fashion, Mustafa's contrapuntal text opens itself to reading the chasms between translation and writing, witnessing and testimony, home and diaspora. In her afterword, Mustafa discusses the work of translation as a process as much of familial collaboration (and striving to understand, even partially, disjunctively) as of composition. Which is not at all to say that coloniality does not intervene in the structuring of these divides, but rather to attend to how it operates

---

3. Edward Said, *Culture and Imperialism* (London: Knopf Doubleday Publishing Group, 2012), 62.

precisely as the cut across which Mustafa joins her line. In the list of "members," a coda as much as an index poised between poems and afterword, Mustafa offers resistant traces of the geographies and names dis/re-membered in processes of translation من اللغة العربية into English torqued against the risk of echoing Zionist efforts to erase the material architecture and cultural memory of Arab life in Palestine. What must be traversed in order to come to tell a history? As Mustafa writes in "dis cord," her opening poem, "I thought / I was Syrian" and "I attempt / my story / on a lost / foundation."

Trish Salah

umbilical discord

dis   cord

2022
bedroom corner
I meet Nazmiyya Al-Kilani
she tells me
>   *the air of* صفد
>   *is salutary for every illness*
and I realize I've been sick
all my life

>   *the house*
>   *is right in front of my eyes*
imagine a Palestine
for myself
>   *I never forget it*
>   *two floors*
>   *an open hall*
in a Syrian courtyard
>   *a garden*
a fountain
>   *two cypresses*
sun and lemon leaf
>   *all flower types*
jasmine bush
>   *imaginable*

I attempt
>   *before the war*
my story
>   *my father wanted to build a third floor*
>   *he already had the stones*

on a lost

and everything prepared
but the war broke out
and he left

foundation

my father had
property

what is
proper?

citrus orchards

improper?

he was
a landlord

and who owns
the tenses?

I attempt

exile

to re cord

my daughter

to re birth

means

to re root

being uprooted

2018
courtyard swing

we had Jewish neighbors
a woman called Um Shimon

I meet Um Khalil
Tetteh's friend
Christian mother

> *Dad gave her a room*
> *to live in*
> *for free*

she bends
over her balcony

> *and what the farmhands*
> *would pick*

she will drop off
grape leaves

> *eggplants*

zucchini

> *tomatoes*

stuffed

> *vegetables*

at sundown

> *he would tell them*
> *"give some to Um Shimon*
> *for free"*

I imagine Syria
a living room

> *we abandoned all the rooms*
> *and lived in the kitchen*
> *sitting under the sink*
> *because of the shooting*

Mama

> *my mother*

and Tetteh

> *didn't live with me*

> *but she came to visit*
> *before my son Issam*
> *was born*

face to face

> *me*
> *my children*
> *my mother*

dismember

> *one day we could manage*
> *to buy bread*

green bean pods

> *but not the next day*

Nazmiyya sighs
shakes her heavy
head

> *what can I*
> *tell you?*

Tetteh's thumb

> *the women of* صفد
> *were like men*

pushes pods

> *like the rebels*
> *they were willing*
> *to carry arms*
> *and fight*

against the blade

> *I used to go on foot*
> *from* صفد
> وادي الطواحين *to*
> *and from there*

back at night
جبل السموعي *to*
muscle memory
    a girl alone

    I became injured when
Tetteh gives up
a broken tale
    I wanted to cross the street
    to escape
"once
a man threatened me
with a knife
    there was a plywood vegetable box
    I broke it apart
    put a piece here
    piece there
I grabbed it
by the blade
    my leg was broken
like this"
    I took my headscarf
    and bandaged my leg

Tetteh weeps for
forgetting
    my mother collapsed
    lost all her strength
Quranic verses
    I carried
    my daughter Bodur
remembers

other ways

> and held the little one
> Issam
> and Anwar could walk

to pray

> I tied him to my apron
> he would look at my leg
> and say

a Palestinian
folk tune

> "Mommy
> blood!
> Mommy
> blood!"

"help us

> "it's nothing
> don't worry"

why did you help me?

> we arrived at the port
> there were ships and boats
> they would grab the kids
> and throw them

you knew I was poor

> some here
> some there

why did you take me?

> the children parted
> from their mothers

by Allah

> I thought we would be gone
> for a short period

for your sake
I'll carry a rifle

>> *and then come back*

and go down to battle

in Marjayoun

>> *from that moment on*
>> *I didn't know*
>> *where your dad was*

help us

>> *the Haganah caught him*
>> *and the youngsters*
>> *who wanted to escape*

help us

>> *and ordered them*
>> *to pick up*
>> *the dead bodies*

the loved ones

have left

>> *they would point*
>> *the Sten gun*

and they didn't bid us

farewell

>> *and tell them*
>> *to pick up*
>> *the bodies*

help us

>> *the war arrived*
>> *in* كا

help us

>> *every young man*
>> *they would find*
>> *armed or not*

may Allah

forgive them
　　　　　they would take
　　　　　to the lighthouse area
how they tortured us"
　　　　　shoot him
　　　　　and throw him
　　　　　to the sea

from the Detroit River
murmurs
　　　　　I asked to talk
　　　　　on the radio
is it enough
　　　　　I said
　　　　　"I
to listen?
　　　　　Nazmiyya Muhyi A-Din Kilani
language
a carrier
　　　　　am looking for
　　　　　my life partner
conveyed
translated
caught
　　　　　I have three children
　　　　　please
over
times
across incommensurable
spaces
　　　　　my Arab brothers and sisters
　　　　　whoever knows whether he is
　　　　　alive

or missed

        or dead

        please

am I grasping
enough?

        inform me through the Red Cross

        I live in the Old City of عكا

        house number eleven sixty-eight"

how do I hold
the raw redness
of a rescue flare?

        by sheer coincidence

        he was sitting in a café at that time

        listening to the radio

of a heart
still beating?

        he jumped up and hugged the radio

        to listen to the rest of the news

and what will this
contact

        "everyone here

        will have coffee on me

        this is my wife speaking

change in me?

        she and my children

        are alive"

        "Mother

        you lived here for sixty years

        all that time thinking

        your brothers and sisters are dead"

I thought
I was Syrian

                    I asked a lot at the Red Cross
                    and made it known through the radio
                    that I was looking for them

until I knew

                    in the end
                    I thought
                    they must have died

host country
is hereditary

                    we were still
                    inside the bus
                    your cousins
                    my brother and my sisters
                    gathered around

but I also know
a courtyard

                    your cousin asked
                    "who in the bus
                    is from the Kilani family?"

a swing

                    Bodur
                    raised her hand

a lemon tree

                    and then
                    everybody burst
                    into the bus

propped up
in memory

                    they lifted
                    Bodur and me up
                    and took us down
                    from the bus

in family

and when they went
up the stairs
they lifted me up

in me

my niece began
to ululate

2001
Nazmiyya
meets her siblings
in Syria

I just miss her
already an ocean away
from the river
from the sea

time is a place
within and
without me

dis   location

أمينة (Amina) / adjective / first name
devoted, honest, straightforward, trusty, believable, loyal,
  faithful

عتابا (Ataba) / noun / last name
plaint or dirge; a traditional Arabic musical form sung at
  weddings, festivals, and other occasions

> *this is* صفورية
> *in the year 1931*

a two-dimensional
distillation

> *I re*
> *member how our land*
> *used to be next to* القسطل
> *in front of* القسطل
> صفورية *at*

all I can build
are half-ruins
somewhere in Syria
Busra Al-Sham
decaying
columns and arches
the shade of
2006

> *I re*
> *member we were having iftar*
> *it was Ramadan*

I know the taste
the collective bite
sun-dried bellies
fast-breaking

        my late father

not "late"
Amina says
حياة ابوي
my living dad

        sat there and my mother
        my mother was pregnant
        and my older living sister Fatema
        and my living brother who was blind

where and when
do the unalived
live?

        this is who I re
        member was there

        إسا *suddenly we heard tanks*
        along the road

إسا or هسا?

        إسا *our land*
        our orchard
        is next to the road

a filler word
tastes like
Falasteen
it means
"now"

        the tanks started shooting
        their sound

I listen for

expired blasts
    wobobob
transcribe
Amina's peddling palms
upholding chaos
    you know
    it's a loud noise
    a roaring
can I
know?

    إسا *my living dad*
    started moving us
my older spine
my sister
searches for
my small body
    to hide
    between the trees
stretched
and still behind
an ancient pillar
    so the Jews
    would not enter
I unhide myself
it is my turn
to seek
    our place

Rama wears Falasteen
around her neck
    my mother told

            my living sister
its sharp perimeter
stitched into
my neurofabric
            she said
            "Fatema يما
            go
            see the family
            of your uncle Hasan Ataba
            have they left already or not?"
internalized outline
imaginary pith
bigger than
my brain
            my living sister goes
            and doesn't find
            my uncle's family
            in their home
an idea
unformed
formative
like a fontanelle
            they'd already left
a soft spot

            إسا *my sister comes back*
            to the orchard
            she doesn't find
            anyone
Rama sketches
Handala
on high school notebooks

                        she went back inside
                        the village
                        into صفورية
faceless boy
with sharp hair
like a child's sun
                        she walked and met
                        my maternal grandfather
                        she tells him
                        "where are my uncle and his wife?"
I know this boy
a good guy
a friend
a familiar
                        he said
                        "dear granddaughter
                        there's nobody left
                        the entire village
                        went away"
Palestine felt like
a past participle
I am trying
to present it

a recent dream
                        everyone started running
Rama among
freedom fighters
                        إسا *she went there*
I'm absent
                        the Jews began shooting at them
                        from the castle

she calls me
I answer

> a bullet hit the palm
> of my living sister's foot

I see it unfold
a film

> إسا there was no one to carry her
> she stayed put

she is driving
and her skin
is melting

> evening came
> and still nobody treated her

terror and love
in her voice

> she lost
> all her blood

the sound
of dying

> I don't know my sister
> I don't know her features

the gravity
of ignorance
pulls in questions

> إسا when I used to visit صفورية

what do I not
know?

> I re
> member that it was here

why do I not
know?

> my living mother told me
> "here's where
> your living sister
> died

do I want to
know?

> she was wearing a dress
> its color
> a light blue"

what has stopped me
from knowing?

> إسا she died
> with her hands in her hair
> pulling

who could
help me to
know?

عارف (Aref) / adjective / grandfather
knowing, knowledgeable, wise, intelligent, sage; Jiddo

حورية (Horiyeh) / noun / grandmother
beautiful young woman, angel, nymph, mermaid; Tetteh

Uncle Hasan tells me
"they were young
but they knew
people came
to Dallata

> إسا the people said
> "we don't want to stay in the orchards

إسا *they will intrude upon us*
and told them
'get out! get out!
the Jews are attacking
with planes and arms
they want to kill
everyone' "

let's go"

this was at night
like a red cloud
news of massacres
reached them

"let's go to نبي قبال
they went
to the Golan
in Al-Qunaitra

it's an area of cactus
and citrus trees
the first
unrooting

the military will not see us
passing"
walking
rhizospheres

we went out
in a wagon
tractor-led
as if this was
a land-clearing
a close-cutting
a harvest

maybe twenty families
or less
I was there

in fragments
written under their skin
an unborn
promise

> *I re*
> *member*

Jiddo
takes my little hand
a graft

> *the children cried all night*
> *we wanted to eat*

a morning
a Ramadan
a Syrian summer
parchment throats

> *we wanted bread*

we bear the sun
to the breadline

> إسا *my living dad*
> *just before dawn*
> *carried a sack of flour*
> *on his shoulder*

a throng
a stone wall window
a wait

> *he told them*
> *"take it*

a token
I swallow

> *go on*
> *get up women*
> *get up and make dough*

            for the kids
with hardship
comes ease
            so they keep quiet
            and go to sleep"
flat yellow
sun discs
droop warm
limp on Jiddo's
forearms
            we ate
            and we enjoyed it
            like we were having lamb
            and everyone slept

            morning came
between a night
            suddenly there was an airplane
and a daybreak
            circling in the air
            circling at a low altitude
the scales
            إسا *we heard through a loudspeaker*
            "clear the area
of the world
            إسا *we will blow it up"*
flip
            we walked to صفورية

            my living dad said
Great-Grandmother

Ghazaleh Awad Hamid
Um Aref

> *"my house is plentiful*
> *but soon*
> *I'll have nothing*
> *left"*

closed
locked
the door

> *when we left*
> *the wooden boxes were ready*
> *loaded with vegetables*

left thinking

> *our dad wanted*
> *to take them to the vegetable market*

they would
return

> *he said*
> *"I'm going to deliver the vegetables*
> *to الناصرة"*

in two or
three days
when things

> *we didn't know*
> *the Jews would come to us*

settled

> *my brother Muhammad*
> *is blind*

"as for the disbelievers

> إسا *my mother said to him*
> *"take Amina*

their deeds are like
a mirage in a desert
and walk from صفورية
towards the orchards
which the thirsty
perceive as water
look for your father
because he hasn't returned yet"
but when they approach it
so we walked
they find it
he led me
down the road
to be
"there"
I told him
"there's Dad"
nothing
he said
"where's Dad?"
instead
they find Allah
I said
"over there
ready to settle
their account
he's asleep"
and Allah
is swift
in reckoning

or their deeds are
like the darkness

       he was afraid

in a deep sea

       I wasn't afraid

covered by
waves upon
waves

       I didn't know
       he was dead

topped by
dark clouds

       he said
       "pick up his hand"

darkness
upon darkness

       I did

if one stretches out
their hand

       he said
       "call him"

they can hardly
see it

       I called
       "يابا يابا"

and whoever Allah
does not bless

       I told Muhammad
       "he's not answering"

with light

       he asks me
       "is there any blood?"

will have

       I said
       "yes"

no light"

24:39-40

>he said
>"where is it?"

the first
blindness

>I said
>"in his head"

delusion

>he said
>"leave him be"

the second

>he didn't want
>to scare me

darkness

>he said
>"leave him be"

I pry

>we walked up the road

my lids

>he started crying

stare

>pinching me
>by Allah

at my palms

>told me
>"cry!
>cry!"

are these

>I said
>"why cry?
>why cry?"

phantom limbs?

>he told me
>"Dad died"

my living mother
was overwhelmed
by pain

the first person
Tetteh birthed
was a girl

she was about
to give birth

they named her
"Amina"

there was no
midwife
there wasn't
anyone

Jiddo cradled
her sunlit
baby breath

my living step-grandmother
was there
Mother said
"Auntie
I'm going to give birth"

but she got
sick

she told her
"what can I do for you
my dear

died

may Allah be with you
what can I do for you"

Tetteh's womb
gutted
hungry
grew twins

my living mother
gave birth
to the girl
alone
at home

the first twin

a corpse

      suddenly
      there was a little baby girl

the second

an omen

      "oh look how pretty she is يما
      يما *what are you going*
      to name her?"

they named her

      "by Allah
      I will call her

"Aisha"

      حربية
      War Baby"

it means

"living"

      what a girl

in time

she will name me

"Rawand"

      what a girl

      we arrived in عيلوط

in the Golan

      no mattress
      no blanket
      no pillow

                    we had nothing
Jiddo's spine
carried
                    we want to live
                    but how will we live?
a rented
house
                    my little living sister was young
                    a baby that needed carrying
and the omen
                    إسا *my living mother*
and Ghazaleh
                    together with another woman
and Great-Aunt Nayfeh
                    called Fatema Al-Marejeh
and Great-Aunt Fatema
                    went to harvest and string
                    the tobacco
and Tetteh
                    among the Bedouins
they ate
land food
                    with the Al-Heib tribe
cheeseweed
dandelions
gundelia
ferula
arum lilies
                    at the village of الحجاجره
collected money
                    by the time they returned
                    in the evening
for a few years
                    they were worn out

by Allah
I had prepared dough

1966

and I started cutting
and flattening it

they bought
a three-dunum land

my mother was working
at the customs office

to build a small
home

suddenly a police force came

three rooms

they were afraid
I'd throw rocks at them

a small field
for planting

so they grabbed my hands
like this

greens
vegetables

the dough was left behind

April 1967

they ruined the dough

they finished
building

they brought in a crane

lived two
months

and lifted the shack up
with the furniture inside

June 1967

they brought in
a truck

Israel attacked
Syria

     and loaded it
     with our stuff
seized the Golan
     they housed us
     inside a store
seized
the home
     an abandoned
     store
forced
another flee
     with scrap metal
Ghazaleh
Nayfeh
Fatema
Jiddo
Tetteh
Aisha
Wahid
Walid
Aida
Hasan
Mama

     damn it
     the homeland
     how dear it is
     damn it
I sit
with Jiddo
     that photo's in صفورية

            around Dad's garden
a fresh night
            يا بيي
            woe to me
in the courtyard
under the lemon tree
            that's our fig tree
            at the edge of the garden
we sip matteh
bitter twigs and leaves
through metal straws
            this is my living husband
Jiddo writes
his book
            and this is me
my little hand
traces dotted lines
            and this is Inas
disjointed
Arabic letters
            and this is my daughter
            who had gotten married
over and over and
            has daughters
over
again

            "where are you going?
            where?
            that's our land"
Amina
a ruffled parrot
speaks in Hebrew

　　　　　　　when he tells you
　　　　　　　"that's our land"
　　　　　　　what can you tell him?

why do I
　　　　　　　by Allah
　　　　　　　once we were sitting
　　　　　　　and I had gas with me

hesitate
　　　　　　　and I would go early in the morning
　　　　　　　take gas with me and eggs and everything
　　　　　　　and have breakfast there
　　　　　　　sometimes lunch

to type
　　　　　　　we would sit down
　　　　　　　we had chairs
　　　　　　　and we had a car

their tongue?
　　　　　　　suddenly he shows up
　　　　　　　saying
　　　　　　　"what are you doing here?"

to transcribe
　　　　　　　my husband
　　　　　　　sitting down
　　　　　　　said
　　　　　　　"what am I doing?"

those foreign
letters?
　　　　　　　he said
　　　　　　　"get out of here
　　　　　　　yalla"
　　　　　　　he asked him
　　　　　　　"why?"

the tongue
　　　　　　　he said

                    "that's our land"
                    in Hebrew
always living
under the same roof
                    he told him
                    "but this is my land here"
malleable
muscle
                    he answered
                    "ahhh
                    go ask your Elohim
with strength
                    we have been here
                    for two thousand years
to tip
                    go away
                    go ask your Lord
the scales
                    up there"

dis   section

I re
member it
inch by inch

2018
Damascus

from all sides
from the beginning

postwar
reunion

of the village
from the beginning

there is no
postwar

of the street
from the spring

only
aftermath

that runs
into the middle

war-warped
life

of the village
this street

ever-expanding
echoes

paved
with small red tiles

the beat
of a billion
butterfly wings

I re
member

Lotfi Al-Ajmi's shop

between the echoes

cherries overflow

Ali Al-Amqawi's shop

spill into

open palms

and plastic bags

Abu Khalil Al-Khatib's shop

Syrians shopping

for sustenance

in open air

souqs

and at the beginning

of the street

elastic ice cream

tamr hindi

bubble machines

Ahmed Aziz Abu Al-Jafra's shop

in Al-Hamidiyah

my mother's cousin

and he was very well-known

punctured tunnel ceiling

feigning stars

he was the one

who used to write and sing

for جفرا

when relatives ask

"where do you prefer?"

across from him

the diwan of Salim Al-Ghadban

the mayor of the village

I echo

Mama

who had a shop

next to his diwan
life in Canada
is comfortable
       as soon as I hear the word
كوبكات
but it's missing
the soul
       my heart
you find
       opens
here

       all the work
       is on the women
Uncle Hasan tells me
       hand in hand
       with the men
that Ghazaleh Um Aref
saw Tetteh
       she rises
       in the night
working the land
in Golan
in Al-Qunaitra
in Jabata Al-Khashab
       and works
       by picking
going and coming
       planting and reaping
filling water
       she is awake
       from six or seven
       in the morning

carrying the sea
on her head

I re
member
Tetteh's hands
   we had three women
soft baked
skin
   went down
knuckle mountains
river veins
   with my mother
   to عكا
deep blue
ink tattoo
on her right wrist
   carrying laban
   three piasters for each jar
striding star
   and عكا *gave her laban*
   for half a piaster
or a dancing flower
   when the morning
   star rose
a shadow
cast by
her ringed finger
   the dairy workers woke
yellowed gold
   and went down
fading sun

polished by passing
down
        to عکا
glows now
on Mama's hand
        my mother
the same
slender fingers
        would often
        grow tired
caring for
ten siblings
        we were seven or eight
        in the house
blessed limbs
        she used to
        knead
vast palms
        cook
to carry
        bake
heavy supplications
        sweep
table spread
        under the carpets
grasp
at life
        she wouldn't finish
teach
life
        until
        sunset
lessons written

in palmar creases

      before the sun
      completely set

made

for movement

      she fell asleep
      from fatigue

for prayer

      in the days of كويكات
      the women would gather firewood
      by themselves

my hands

      they would wake

bear witness

      up at four in the morning
      to go to جدين

to this story

      and when they came back
      to كويكات

to the hands

      the firewood bearers
      would throw down

that have borne

      their load

before me

"tell me Mama
about the twins"

      there was no such thing
      as a pregnant woman

"I felt good
to be like

my mother

       all of them were working
       people used to give birth
       at home

twins are
hereditary

       and there was nothing easier
       than giving birth

I was the only one
among my sisters
to become pregnant
with twins

       she didn't groan

everything was normal

       unless she was giving birth

until the fifth month

       there were women
       who gave birth

I saw doctors
throughout the pregnancy
the babies were fine

       among the firewood
       or while they were picking olives

but my belly
wasn't so big

       one of us gave birth

once

       in the land of الطيونه

I was coming home
our neighbor was sitting

       to this day
       no one has called her Suhaila
       only طيونه

up on the balcony
she said
'I heard you're pregnant
with twins
is it true?

        the women
        used to walk
        a lot

by Allah
you don't even look pregnant
with one baby

        and the baby
        would always
        be turning

judging
by how fast
you walk

        not like today

as if you're not pregnant
at all'

        everyone gives birth
        by operations

in that instant
I felt pain
in my back

        why?

the pain of a woman
about to give birth

        from too much sitting
        the baby doesn't turn

I had given birth before

        doesn't move

I knew the feeling"

2013
Windsor
living room

with the first attack

Mama started
screaming

the Jews approached
from west of the village

a wailing
siren

from the seas
at night

"they took Rafe!

before dawn

they took Rafe!

they attacked
the village

he's gone
it's over

and the people
of the village
responded

start praying
for your uncle

praise be to Allah

they're going to
kill him

they were not able
and withdrew

for Allah's sake

and maybe
some of them
were killed

get me on the phone
with whoever
is in charge
>   because we saw traces
>   of blood and dirt
and let me speak
to Rafe
>   in the morning
O my life
O my soul"
>   between the plants
I wept with Rama
struck and dumb

"tell me Mama
what happened
to Rafe?"
>   the second attack
>   was after the armistice
"one day
he went with Maiar
to pick up his wife from work
in Al-Fadel
>   the Jews attacked us
>   at night
>   from نهاريا
an area full
of different
Syrian rebel groups
>   and started attacking
>   the village
>   with cannons

the regime
surrounded the area
      I re
      member that it was the first day
      of Ramadan
no one
could leave
there were snipers
on the roofs
      we fled
      from كويكات
      ابو سنان *to*
they attacked
destroying people
rocks
everything
      كفر ياسيف *and*
      and to the mountains
Maiar
was four
      and in the morning
they ran
from shelter to
shelter
      my aunt returned
his wife told me
on the phone
that the government forces
caught Rafe
      to كويكات
which meant
he wouldn't
return

51

and they
killed her
that was the last thing
I heard before she
hung up

before the truce began
we lost hope
we went with my parents
to جت
the regime's method
was to gather all the men
and then we went
to لبنان
to my mother's family
Rafe lined up
with the rest
and when the month of the truce came
my dad said
the commander collected IDs
before ordering the gunman
to shoot
"come on يابا
let's go back
to the village
it was
Rafe's turn
the village is full
of people
the commander
paused

                    and the wind
                    has blown away
                    all the hay
'where do I
know you from?'
                    and there is nothing
                    but wheat left
'yesterday night
my cousin and I caught
people stealing
and we came to you
to report them'
                    come on
                    we are going
                    to go back
                    to the village"
'take your ID
and get out of here'
                    we rode on the Beast
                    at sunset
Rafe fled
stepping over
his friends'
corpses
                    we went down
                    from رميش
                    from دير القاسي
                    to جدين
returned to his wife
and son
                    at dawn call to prayer
                    we arrived at كويكات
and escaped"

"Mama

      we didn't have anything
      except for some bread

I think
I'm beginning
to understand

      and when the month of the armistice ended
      the Jews attacked the people

why Palestine
is peripheral

      and the people left
      my Lord
      as if newly created
      by You

how could we
hold on
to a receding
horizon

      the one who had cows
      left them
      and the one who had fowl
      left them
      all tied with ropes

when rushing waters
demand we grasp
at the straws
before us?"

      we walked until we reached جت
      and in جت *we sat*

"indeed
my daughter

      under the olive trees
      in the east
      at the pond

we get caught up
with the problems
at our feet

> *for about a month*
> *people of* كويكات
> *people of* عمقا
> *people of* السامرة

even for you
what happened in Syria
is told to you
in stories

> *people used to say*
> *"we're going to leave*
> *our village*

we lack
intimacy
with Palestine

> *either for seven days*
> *or seven months*
> *or seven years"*

we haven't drunk
from her waters

> *and here we are*
> *we still haven't*

it all depends
on where you've made

> *returned*

your memories"

Mama tells me
"Rafe's wife
worked in a pharmacy
in Al-Fadel

the first time
we got out of the village
and whenever there were fights
between the regime
and the rebels
my mother took the Beast
from ابو سنان
they would help
the wounded
no matter which side
they belonged to
and left to bring wheat
so that we could grind it
and eat
but to help a rebel
was to be a rebel
and while she was in كويكات
she met two men
wearing blue shirts
the spies knew Rafe
but they knew him
as Abu Maiar
so it took a while
to track him down
they saw her
looking around for someone
they sent for him
to be tried
in the Criminal Security Department
where the one who enters
seldom leaves"
to help her carry the wheat

Mama talked with
her friend's husband
an army colonel
                    they pitied her
"please
we don't want Rafe
to go alone"
                    and went down to help
he went down with him
to make sure he got out
                    Allah knows
                    if they were Arabs or Jews
they interrogated him
asked what
and how
and why
                    they brought her the flour
released him
after twelve hours
                    and packed the wheat
the colonel told him
                    and said to her
"my advice to you
                    "*go*
leave the country
                    and don't return
they're going to keep
bringing you in
and releasing you
bringing you in
and releasing you
                    if you return

Allah knows
if one time
they'll bring you in
        the Haganah
        will shoot you"
and you won't end up
leaving"

        عكا *went*
Tetteh left Safad
        and حيفا *fell*
for Syria
        people feared for their lives
        and fled in panic
oblivious
of the future
        had we stayed
        in our village
fragmentation
        we would have been killed
        immediately
of her womb

        the war came to us
"I felt the pain
        from the direction
        of نهاريا
in my back
        they started throwing
        hand grenades
I went to the doctor

               to try
               to scare us
Allah have mercy on him
they tell me he died
               we stopped
               being
I went to him
in the afternoon
               able to see
he tested me
               in front of us
he said
'you're right
               when I saw the war
               about to begin
something's wrong

you have symptoms
               I had two children
of giving birth
               Hussein
               four years old
contractions'
               and Hasan
               a year and a half
he gave me
medication
               I wasn't afraid
               for myself
said we should keep
an eye on things
               but the shelling

from that moment
                    made me fear
my belly
                    for my children
started to grow
                    I said to myself
quickly
                    "where can I take them?
quickly
                    where could I hide them?"
quickly
                    I said to myself
filling up
                    "I'll put them
with water
                    in the attic

                    but what if
                    the attic
                    falls?"

at the start
of the seventh month
my belly grew
as if I was in the tenth
                    I said
we went
to many doctors
it was
a strange case
                    "If I put them
                    below the attic

no solution
                    the same
                    problem
the doctor said
he had to be present
at the very second
of birth
to break the water
let it out
bit by
bit
                    the possibility that
if the water escaped
all at once
air would enter
my body
                    the attic
and stop
my heart
                    might fall
                    on them"

they prepared
the operating room
brought extra blood
it was urgent
it was
time
                    it was
                    a large wooden trunk
he tried to let out
all those liters
of water

bit by
bit
in a huge
bucket

I put
the children
inside

suddenly
all the water
escaped at once
drenching
his body overflowing
the bucket

and closed

he cried for
help this was
the scenario he feared

the lid

'push!
push!
push!'

but Hussein

the first baby
came out
she was alive

got right up

but she quickly
died

burst out the box

the second
stayed inside

and said

I was

drained
wanted to sleep
had to stay awake
        "Mother
'push!
push!
push!'
        يما
she suffocated
        you're suffocating us"
inside

        O woe
        is me
they buried them
under the dirt
        what they did
        to us
I wallowed
in postpartum
        praise be to Allah
a lonely
suffering
        for what He has written
people came
to celebrate
my recovery
        I called Abu Hussein
        and told him
but I was
childless
        "you carry Hussein

and leave

you can forget

the pain

> *from the western part*
> *of the village*

when you look over

and see your babies

> *I'll take Hasan with me*
> *and follow you*

but without them

> *there"*

it was

pain

> *I removed*
> *my white head cover*
> *to not be seen*
> *from its whiteness*

on top

of pain"

> *and shot at*

2021

Damascus

> *we came to*
> *Suleiman Ziada's house*
> *in* ابو سنان

a rented home

> *three months*

full of

Canadians

> *then* لبنان

Qataris

> قانا

Dutch

       صور
       a whole year

Swedes

       back to ابو سنان

Syrians

       to the sheikhs

French

       of the Khair family

Americans

       their homes full
       of deported people

Palestinian
patchwork

       the Saad family
       took us in

"since then

       if I don't return
       to كويكات

every time I visited

       my son will
       return

the doctor

       what are you
       talking about?

I found him holding
a highlighter

       enough

studying

       let me do the talking

saying

       do you see this street

'I'm still studying
your case

        that goes to نهاريا?

we have never
come across
anything

        everything they took
        from our land

like it

        in كويكات

I don't know

        the day will come

what happened
to you

        Allah willing

what to call it

        while we're alive

where the water

        and we will return
        to the village

came from'

        and if I don't return

it must have been

        my son will return

the evil eye

he was the doctor who
delivered you too

        my older brothers
        died in لبنان

it was difficult

        my nephew
        died in القاسمية

to think

> *my brother's wife*
> *died in* البازوريه

of having kids

> *her husband*
> *died in* قطر

again

> *my other brother's son*
> *died in* استراليا

it took

> *my other brother*
> *died in* برج البراجنة

time

> *and my nephew and his son*

but my faith

> *hit by a shell*
> *in* بيروت

is strong

> *and they died*

Rama was in
the second grade

> *everyone died*
> *in a different place*

six or seven
years old

> *but their children*
> *remain*

two years later

> *and they still*
> *demand*

you were born"

> *to return*

dis   ease

           the one
           who gave birth
"life
in the midst
of death"
           would rest
           for a week
Aunt Maesa's tale
in Facebook posts
2014
           they would
           feed her
"people say
'they've reached Sweden!
           the best food
lucky them!'
           some would be
           pampered
but they don't know
how we arrived
           and rest
           for longer
what happened to us
to arrive
           they'd say
           "the puerperium's grave
           is open for forty days"
what we
endured
to arrive
           others
           with families
the story began
last year

when my husband
started looking

        what could they do?

for a way
to travel abroad
to improve our
conditions

        they had to take care
        of the family

and the future
for our children

        I re
        member

the story began
last year

        once
        after the occupation

after we left Syria

        my grandmother
        used to harvest wheat

hoping
after a few months
to return

        I pitied her

the situation in the country
deteriorated more
and more

        and went
        to help her

we stayed
in Egypt

>   *while I was pregnant*
>   *with Maurice*

the situation
much worse

>   *I went to lift*
>   *the pile of wheat*

conditions tight
intensified suffering
without
exception

>   *are you*
>   *recording this?*

psychologically
financially
socially
morally
and
and
and

>   *when I felt something*
>   *smooth*

until my husband
began to convince
himself and me
to travel to Sweden
by sea

>   *a coiled snake*

I was completely against
this crazy idea

>   *I jolted*

he would go
alone

>   *and screamed*

how would I
remain alone
in a strange country?

> *my mother*
> *came running*

how would
the children
accept the idea?

> *"what's wrong*
> يما?*"*

rumination
took
our comfort
strained
our nerves
disturbed
our lives

> *"يما*
> *it's a snake"*

it's a
very difficult
decision

> *my brother*
> *came and*
> *killed it*

more difficult
than you can
imagine

> *what a snake!*

we agreed
to travel
with him

> *about a meter*

                    and a half
                    long
everyone wanted us
to leave
                    curse it
                    how smooth it was!

the time
had come!
                    the Jews attacked us
                    at night
very quickly
the news came
to get ready
                    we locked
                    the house
                    with the key
we informed
my sister Aida
who gathered people
in Syria
to read Surah Yasin
                    and we went out
with the intention
of facilitating
the trip
                    we thought
                    we would go
                    to the mountain
among them my sister Nisreen
who didn't know for whom
she was praying

and the second day
we would
return

we didn't tell her
because of her
excessive
tenderness

I heard shooting
in the village

we turned off
our phones

we left صرعة
at night

and took
vertigo pills

we went towards
the train station
in عرتوف

they took us
in a bus
with other
Syrians

we were dropped off
in the mountains
opposite the village

exhaustion
extreme heat
disturbance
boredom

the Jews occupied
the village

we prayed
prayed to Allah

and in the morning

we reached
the sea

they destroyed it
while we
watched

all the Syrians
were there

I saw and heard
how they destroyed

families
children
infants
young people
elderly who couldn't
walk

our homes

I couldn't cry
from dizziness
and fatigue

they would place
explosives in them
and detonate them

the children
were hungry
and thirsty

explosions and
explosions

smugglers came
and advised people
to return

for two days

but the sword

preceded
the blame

while we
listened

the point came
of no return

people began
to go to villages

the wave
was high

instead of staying
in the mountains

the smuggler warned us
against causing
chaos

we went to
زكريا

but everyone attacked
the ferries

some went
to بيت نتيف

as if they were
rescue boats

and some went
to بيت عطاب

as is usual for us
Syrian people

the people
scattered

my husband
started saving children
who fell in the water

we walked

whatever
I describe
will be unable
to describe
the description

       بيت نتيف
       was full
       of refugees

everyone in the boat
stagnant and stunned
everyone on the shore
thinking of whether
to return or
continue

       we built
       a pergola
       from tree branches
       stayed there
       for two months

the children cried
and screamed

       we went
       to زكريا
       stayed in a
       cave

my husband carried Tarek
on his shoulders
grabbed Malak
with his hand

       the whole village
       full of people
       displaced

reached the boat

running
> *from many*
> *villages*

by Allah
I don't know how
I ran in the water
the waves nearly
drowning us
> *from our*
> *village*

all I felt
was someone
raising me
throwing me
in the ferry
> *from* عرتوف
> *from* إشوع
> *and* عسلين

we reached
the expected boat
in the sea
> *we stayed there*
> *a month*

the sailors
cooperated
to pull us in
> *there was an attack*
> *on* زكريا

my heart
stopped
almost
> *like the attack*
> *that happened to us*

in صرعة

people
flocked

we went up
to the mountains

climbed in
the boat

the same way we did
when we left
our village
when they occupied

زكريا

stationed
themselves

some people
didn't leave their homes
they didn't leave
in time

they said
women and children
could go down
below

we lived
in a house
with fifteen families

we went down
our feet unable
to carry us

at night
we rode a truck

we just wanted
to sleep
it was three in the morning

from بيت أولا
to سعير

we were
shocked

    the driver
    dropped us off

'what
is this?'

    in a place
    we didn't know

nothing like what
they described
to us

    and in the morning
    we saw that

this is

    it was

a storehouse
for fish

    a dumpster

without
any room
to breathe

the journey
of a thousand miles
began

    when we got out
    of ترشيحا

we lost a day
and a half
at sea

                    we weren't aware
                    of anything
waiting for
another boat
                    the first raid
                    took place
                    at five in the morning
to bring
food and
                    I was about
                    to knead some flour
                    so that we could
                    take bread with us
water
                    my father
                    drinking coffee
the boat
arrived
                    suddenly
                    Abu Mahmoud Al-Hawari
                    entered our house
carrying supplies
                    he ran
                    and shouted
                    "our house
                    is gone"
and more than
one hundred people
                    his sister Fawzia
                    who was in my class
                    wasn't burned
we were already
about one hundred

and seventy
              but when
              Kamel's wife and son
              were brought out
              they were burned
not including
the children
              many people died
              in the raid
              about eighteen
we were at a loss
as to where
those people
would sit
              a thirteen-year-old
              pregnant girl
              jumped out
              the window
we refused
to go down
to the bottom
              people came
              wrapped her in a blanket
              and carried her
to the hellish
space
              we didn't have time
              to bury the bodies
preferred to sleep
in the cold
              Fatema Al-Hawari
              was under
              the debris

rather than die
                    she called
                    to the ones
                    removing the
                    rubble
of suffocation
                    "come further
                    here
                    a little below
                    and be careful"
in the collective
coffin

                    the Jews entered
                    and took the lands
no room
for movement
                    by force
neither the old
nor the young
could purify themselves
                    they closed
                    the mosque
                    and let no one
                    enter
and thus we couldn't fulfill
the most important task
                    I would read Quran
                    on my children
prayer
and reading Quran
                    to protect them

despite this

in تل عراد

there were
young men

we were
severely
tormented

may Allah
protect them

until we got
water

who got up early
in the morning

we used to travel

at a time when
there was no
crowding

long distances

and they cooperated
to perform ablution
in the sea

and go up
mountains

putting a foot down
to wash it
while on the brink
of falling

to search
for water

sometimes
young men
held on to the one
performing ablution

> *they cut*
> *the water supply*

all the while
our blood drying up

> *and demolished*
> *the wells*

in our veins
from worry

> *by Allah*
> *my throat*
> *is dry*

I will try
to gather
my thoughts

> *every time*
> *we bring up*
> *the topic*
> *of the village*

as much as
possible

> *my throat*
> *dries up*

they are

> *from*
> *agitation*

lost and
scattered

> *the revolutionaries*
> *and mujahideen*

when it came
to the food

used to come
to the Christians
for food

it was
shameful

they used to enter
with their muddy boots

anyone who had food
hid it

the headquarters
of the Arab Liberation Army
was based near the pool

whenever the sailors
came to distribute
the food

this army
did nothing
but eat
and drink

jam
bread
dates
cheese
canned
meat

its soldiers
used to give their clothes
to the people
to wash them

I will not
be able
to describe

when we were young
I used to hear about people
accused of treason

the fights
and quarrels

they used to bring them
from عكا and حيفا
to ترشيحا

and 'I got my share'
and 'I didn't get mine'

and imprison them
in the well

and each one
climbed over
the other

they used to
lower food
down to them

and raised
their voices

there was someone
from عكا

and we sat
looking at these
pests

who entered our house
from below

my eyes
shedding tears
for this sick nation

started to
vomit blood

what happened to us
happened for a reason
                they said
                this was because
                he was imprisoned
no one loves
anyone
                the revolutionaries
                were the ones
                imprisoning them
and no one
likes good
for anyone
but themselves
                I re
                member once
we began to pray
to Allah
                they accused Rakad Al-Geshi
                of the intention
not to take us
to account
                to sell his land
                to the Jews
for what
the foolish among us
did
                they took him
                and killed him
and we began
to say to them
'shame on you

              once
              Israelis stepped hard
              on Abu Sami Bishara's
              hand
people are dying
and being killed
in our country
              until it
              broke
and instead of uniting
we are unable
to cooperate
              while they
              were pushing him
              at the gate
in the midst
of death
              they did this
              to make him confess
              that he was
              a revolutionary
with nothing around us
except water
              I re
              member my father and I
              were sitting
              drinking coffee
and the mercy
of our Lord
              the Arab army
              started walking
              next to the house

and how
can we ask
for mercy

> *my father asked*
> *"what's wrong?"*

when we have
no mercy
for each other?'

> *they didn't reply*

it was as if
we were talking
to ourselves

> *he told them*
> *"go*
> *may Allah*
> *never bless you"*

our psyche
deteriorated

> *then my father said*
> *"it's over*
> *it's ruined"*

more and
more

> *the next day*
> *the planes came*
> *and struck*
> ترشيحا

by Allah Almighty

> *we used to walk at night*
> *and by day*
> *we put rocks under our heads*
> *and slept beneath the olives*

whenever I looked
at the sea
                I picked bags of olives
                and thyme
I used to think
and meditate
and fear Allah
and say
                woe to us
'what is this
that we have done?'
                where are our
                belongings?
it is a sight
that terrifies
                where are our
                belongings?
the soul
a boat
                will we
                or won't we
                return?
in the heart
                by Allah's will
                we will return
                to our village
of the sea
                by Allah
                even if I had
                a villa here
nothing
around it
                I would still
                return

set up a tent
and stay in it

no human

stay here?

no animal

stay

no object

a refugee?

I closed
my eyes

the people here
call us
refugees

unable
to look

this is the place
of refugees

for more than
a few moments

it's difficult
to be called
a refugee

glory be
to Allah

by Allah
it's difficult

the painful situation

we would fight
with a Yemeni Jewish guard

was that we only had
four small water bottles left

I asked him
"what are you doing here?"
for the children
he said
"I cut up the pigs
under the olive trees"
so we decided
to bring our bags
from the bottom
we were
six women
to keep them
in front of our eyes
we'd go together
and surround him
for fear
of theft
once
imagine with me
he called me
and started saying
that we are in the middle
of the unknown
of the sea
"come
see what the Arabs
did in my room
and thefts
can happen
they stole things
and flipped
the table"
indeed

ten water bottles
in our friends' bags
were stolen

> *I told him*
> *"they unhinged*
> *and stole a door*
> *but you stole*
> *the villages"*

and here
the words
fell silent

then came our date
with death
in the middle
of the fifth day

> *the Jews came*

we thought
a rescue ship arrived

> *and gathered the village*

suddenly
without warning
the sailors fled
madly

> *on the mountain*

a crazy speed

> *they stopped the tanks*
> *put three machine guns on them*
> *and aimed them at the people*
> *sitting in the valley*

and soon the sea
went crazy

>   *from seven in the morning*
>   *to two in the afternoon*
>   *the world was ablaze*

in every sense
of the word

>   *"either leave*

and here
I don't think I can
describe
what it was

>   *or the whole village*
>   *will be killed"*

but I will do my best
because I made a covenant
with Allah

>   *by Allah*

if I had more life

>   *the pregnant*
>   *woman*

to live

>   *had a stillborn*
>   *from fear*

I would write
everything

>   *they put people in trucks*
>   *and sent them to Gaza*

we leaned
on the side of the boat

>   *and after they*
>   *deported people*

the speed

unfathomable
>   *they sat*
>   *in their place*
>   *and told us to go*
>   *to the mountain*

and the ship
still watching us
but from afar
>   *"whoever we see tomorrow*
>   *at eight in the morning*
>   *we will slaughter"*

they likely realized
we were on our way
to perishment
>   *civilians were running*
>   *barefoot*
>   *blood oozing*
>   *from their feet*

so they did not
advance
>   *we stayed*
>   *in* اللقيه

and moved away
from us
>   *the mukhtar said*
>   *"stay where you are*

but the sea
grew madder
>   *surrender the village*

the world
growing dark
and cold

              if you surrender
              we will give you
              identities
my husband
sat in front of us
taking strong waves
on his back
              surrender
to protect us
              for the sake
              of your homeland
but the waves
overpowered him
and reached us
              for the sake
              of your children"
and the children
shivered
              they gave us
              identities
I covered them
to no avail
              they forced my father
              out of his house
              and demolished it
the darkness
set
              the sky
the sea
              turned red
boiled
and boiled
              from the shooting

                        and the fire
waves rising
more than ten meters
                        all this
                        to frighten people
throwing us to the top
throwing us to the bottom
                        they started
                        beating people
and prayers
roaring in the sea
                        to make them carry
                        their belongings
                        on their backs
voices raised
with mercy
                        they broke
                        someone's hand
we took to reading
Quran
                        started saying
                        to him
and supplications
                        "come on
                        carry!
we did not leave
a supplication
that we knew
                        carry!"
except that we
repeated it
                        they forced him
                        to carry things

over and
over again

       with his broken
       hand

the sailors said
'just pray!
pray to Allah'

       they carried us

by Allah

       from اللقيه

my voice

       تل عراد *to*

disappeared

       they massacred
       six people
       in the Sharia Council

and there were those
who cried

       to frighten people
       and deport them

those
who prayed

       they killed
       the men

those
who slept

       they burned
       the houses

those
who stared

       they burned

the crops
and those
who ate!
        when we fled
by Allah
there were people
only concerned with
eating and drinking
        my mother
        forgot the cooking
        on the fire
while we were
bidding farewell
to each other
        my father dragged me
        by the hand
I grabbed
my children
        my uncle Ahmed
        held on to
        a chain
from the lifejacket belt
with determination
        my hair
        was stuck
        to the chain
so that if we fell
into the water
we would stay
together

Malak couldn't sleep
but raised her head

and screamed at people
   ah
   what do we do?
'make supplications!
why are you silent?
   here we are
   we're going
   to die
I'm going
to supplicate
   يا بيي
   ولا
   الله اكبر
O Allah
stop the waves
   who wouldn't
   want to return
   to their village?
O Allah
answer me
   who wouldn't
   want to return
   to their home?
why isn't He
answering me?
   to their village
   to their land?
isn't the wave
a servant of Allah?
   how did our fate
   turn like this?
why doesn't it
stop?'
   we were

        living

I kissed her

        we had
        everything

I hugged her

        everything
        in our lands

tried to
calm her

        Allah be praised
        what can we do?

she told me
'don't be silent

        when I went
        to the plantations

Mama
pray'

        I couldn't recognize
        a single stone

I told her
'lower your voice

        not even one
        this small

my love
Allah hears you'

we bade farewell
to our children

        the soldiers
        dragged my children
        and me

apologized
to them

they told us
to walk
and began shooting
at our feet

because we could not
provide

we went down
to a spring nearby

what we
wished for

I sat on a rock
placed my daughter
at my nipple
and fed her

could not
fulfill our promises
to them

my son rested
under a tree
the snow fell
without stopping

perhaps
what Allah has
is better

my children asked
"Mama
are we going
to die?"

and more
merciful

I answered
"all praise
is to Allah"

I was holding
my mother's cloak
in my hands
> we sat among
> the trees

her prayer beads
> my mother had made me
> a beaded purse

a bag
she gave me
> I hung it
> up in the olive tree

I smelled it
and said
'the fate of this cloak
was to accompany me'
> but the next morning

I apologized
to my mother
> I forgot it

and held her cloak
before it fell
> and it stayed
> hanging

into the sea
> in the olive tree

I prayed
for my siblings
and spoke to them
> I know about
> the children
> hiding in a

                    chicken coop
and I prayed
for my mother
                    and their mother
and asked my Lord
to make her
pleased with us
                    hiding
                    under the bed
and I saw my father
                    and their father
as usual
coming to me
                    hiding in a barrel
                    the lid shut
in times of adversity
                    the Jews arrived
                    and shot the children
I told him
'our meeting
has neared'
                    while their mother
                    watched

by Allah
                    they started
                    shooting people
by Allah
                    the Jews
                    killed my cousin
                    on the road
                    to غزة
by Allah

they shot Haj Khalil
and cut off his fingers
I could hear the sea
roaring
        a tank came
as if it was asking us
for food
        and killed people
        as they were going
        to غزة
Malak asked me
'what's that sound?'
        they shot
        the elderly Sheikh Qaddoura
I answered
'the sea
        while he was sitting
        and praying
glorifies Allah'

everyone strained
        everyone worked
their eyes
        picking olives
        harvesting
that they might
see a light
from afar
        we'd ride the camel
        carry the plants on it
whenever a light

appeared on the horizon
                    we used to say
they screamed
                    "the moon
'there's a light
they've come to save us!'
                    always walks
                    with us"
but it was only
the light of the moon
                    why isn't the moon
                    bright anymore?
appearing suddenly
from afar
                    we used to stay up
                    with the light of the moon
and disappearing
again
                    the night
                    black as kohl
and here I learned
the true meaning
                    without growing
                    fearful
of the parable
of the drowned man
                    until the English
                    started gathering us
clinging
to straw
                    searching
                    for weapons

my supplications
stopped

are you headed
to our village?

but in my heart
I said
'O Lord

send peace
upon my village

my strength
has failed

it is where I want
to die

and I wish
to sleep

"by Allah's will

and wake

you will
live there"

either on land
or in the sky' "

re   cord

2001

                    I went to امريكا

we land
in Canada

                    I didn't enjoy it
                    I'm only happy
                    in ترشيحا

Damascus
recedes

                    I'm only comfortable
                    in ترشيحا

un
war torn

                    it's my village
                    I was born
                    here

am I
still

                    and I hope
                    to die here

a refugee?

                    by Allah
                    I don't know
                    when I was born

these Palestinian
grandmothers

                    we left
                    when I was fifteen
                    how long have we been
                    gone?

doubt their
birthdays

look at my body
would you believe
I'm seventy-six years old?

approximate
their age

I carried so many loads
on my head

odd
uneven
estimations

it keeps you
energized

measure age
in energy

I haven't
grown old

then again

when I went
to امریکا

birthdays depend
on witness

they asked me

and no one re
members

"how old are you?"

the first taste
of oxygen
in our throats

they didn't
believe me

the first
umbilical cord
severance

ترشيحا
had many
poor people

I daydream

but all people
were helping each
other

of a different
childhood

with love
not like
today

a different
vocabulary

no one helps each
other

no غربة
exile

no لم الشمل
reunion

they hire people
to take care of
the elderly

even the sweetness
of reunion

visiting teachers would say
"we went to many villages

mixes instantly
with the anticipation
of rupture

but this village is so sweet
its rocks are sugar"

dissolves

2018
Damascus

when we used to go
to حيفا or عكا

the courtyard swing
beneath me

we didn't sleep
from joy

a pendulum

we had
fig vineyards

the lemon tree
above me
a witness

and my grandmother

Tetteh

used to make
a pergola

beginning
to forget

and sleep
on top of it

I
beginning
to re
member

with my
younger siblings

listening
to Great-Aunt Nayfeh
a furrowed brow
speak about Falasteen

```
                    to protect
                    the figs
                    from theft
Jiddo
                    my father
                    used to sleep
in his grave
                    in the apple vineyard
an unfathomable
space
                    below


what is it
that moved me
                    the first time
                    I saw my sisters again
                    was in '79
                    when we went to قبرص
to trace
this umbilical
re cord?
                    you don't want to know
                    what happened
                    when I saw them
to shed my
ignorance
                    my elder sister
                    came out of the car
                    and I recognized her
                    somebody else came out
masked
```

and sat down next to me
she said
"how are you?"

by innocence?

and she started kissing me
I told her
"first tell me

I dig through
my Stories Archive

whose daughter are you?"

May 6
2021
"Israeli forces invade Palestinian home
in Sheikh Jarrah neighborhood of
occupied Jerusalem"

everyone there
cupped their faces
in their hands
and told me

#savesheikhjarrah
#gazaunderattack
#freepalestine

"this is your sister!"

I found Palestine
in the palm
of my hand

I couldn't speak
a word

2021
Damascus

          I re
          member weddings were
          a joyous spectacle
I befriend Aunt Aida
a poet whose name means
"returning"
          when I got married
          I rode a decorated horse
she takes me
          they took me
          to the water well
to an art exhibition
          my paternal cousins
          standing on one side
          my maternal cousins
          on the other
          singing
a room of wisps
and colorful geometry
          I forgot
          the songs
a headless man plays the oud
one hand alive
one blue
          they put candles
          in my hands
floating hands
wield a slingshot
over a poppy field
          my wedding
          only eight months
          before the displacement

a rooster crows
a clear song
above a dead dove

Aida writes
"he is the great artist
Ali Jarwan
I had the honor to visit
                on our way
عين الأسد *to*
his last exhibition
in Damascus
                we found
on the walls
                under an olive tree
extended the curves
of love
                a girl from عيلبون
for the land
and the soil
and the orchards
                a pink blanket
                wrapped around her
I read in it
the sadness and joy
of the intentions
                and next to her was a bag
                containing
the prayers of mothers
                clothes
                an empty milk bottle
and the singing

of the swallows

  and a pacifier

  was in her mouth

I smelled the fragrance of

  my mother

  could not carry her

steadfastness

resistance

and determination

  with us

to return

  because she was carrying

  my brothers

with your likes

the country is proud

and exalts itself

with glory and honor

  but when we arrived

  between بيت جن *and* عين الأسد

I wish you all the success

and brilliance

  she saw an old woman

  returning from بيت جن

  and crying

and I'm grateful

for your kind and valuable gift

  she asked us

  if we saw a girl on our way

  we told her

  yes

which I heard sing and say

'in the shadow of the country

you are a country

and we told her
where
you are a house whose door
is the curvature of absence
but when she went
she didn't find the girl
you are a sky
swallows wandering in its blue
maybe the army nearby
took her
you are the amorous orange vines
we asked the old lady
why her mother tossed her
you are the return of childhood
to the clouds
she told us
you are the shadow
of the shadow embracing peace
"her mother
was holding a child
on her back
with scarves that rise above
the peaks of time
and a child
in her arms
you are the silence
and speech in the country
and she could not bear
the weight"
whose shadow is inhabited
by love and light' "

2021
Damascus
Yarmouk Camp
    our village
    had two cemeteries
we arrive
at the cemetery
for an Eid visit
    after the displacement
Uncle Rafe
Uncle Zafer
Uncle Hasan
Uncle Walid
Aunt Aisha
Aunt Aida
Aunt Maesa
Aunt Nisreen
Mama cursing
under her breath
    Ahmed Said Karroum from الفراضية
    passed away
we search for Tetteh and Jiddo
among the debris
of white tombstones
blank or broken
hiding in a yellow sea
of grass
    and when we went to bury him
    in the cemetery of كفر عنان
we watered
the resting places
planted green branches
to supplicate for the dead

         the Israeli military governor
         came and prevented us
         and we went to trial
         until a member of an Arab church
         intervened

O Allah

grant them spacious graves

and fill them with light

         and we pledged
         that this would be the last time
         we would bury someone there

they've left the wreck

we're living in

         neither the living nor the dead
         returned

"Al-Fatiha"

         I wasn't born
         in لفتا

I stare at the ruins

of Yarmouk

         my memories

uninhabited streets

bullet holes in cement

missing chunks

of wall and roof

empty window frames

         are what my mother and father
         used to tell me

buildings like

unfinished clay projects

         about their life there

concrete slipping
off iron skeletons

       when I go to القدس
       I sometimes go
       to see لفتا

a frozen state
of half-fall

       I don't go down
       I look down

I fixate on
a crumbling building

       I see it from above
       and it's very beautiful

with a cavernous hole

       I never went down

in the middle of its face

       because I didn't have the courage
       to go alone

a mouth agape
a sinister laugh

       I don't know
       anyone there

telling me
to carry belonging
on my back

       next time
       I hope to go down

Mama tells me
"this is the hospital
in which you were born"

       I will tell you the story
       from the beginning

mem bers

نظمية الكيلاني	Nazmiyya Al-Kilani
صفد	Safad
فلسطين	Palestine
سوريا	Syria
ام شمعون	Um Shimon
ام خليل	Um Khalil
تيتة حورية	Tetteh Horiyeh
ماما	Mama
عصام	Issam
وادي الطواحين	Wadi Al-Tawahin
جبل السموعي	Mount Al-Sammu'i
بدور	Bodur
أنور	Anwar
مرجعيون	Marjayoun
عكا	Acre
نهر ديترويت	Detroit River
أمينة عتابا	Amina Ataba
صفورية	Saffuriyya
القسطل	Al-Qastal
بصرى الشام	Busra Al-Sham
فاطمة	Fatema
راما	Rama
حسن عتابا	Hasan Ataba
حنظلة	Handala
جدو عارف	Jiddo Aref
خالو حسن	Uncle Hasan
دلاتة	Dallata
نبي قبال	Nabi Qabal

الجولان	Golan
القنيطرة	Al-Qunaitra
تيته غزالة عوض حميد (ام عارف)	Tetteh Ghazaleh Awad Hamid (Great-Grandmother Um Aref)
الناصرة	Nazareth
محمد	Muhammad
آمنة	Amina
حربية	Harbiyya
خالتو عائشة	Aunt Aisha
روند	Rawand
عيلوط	Ilut
عمتو نايفة	Great-Aunt Nayfeh
فاطمة المريجة	Fatema Al-Marhagi
عمتو فاطمة	Great-Aunt Fatema
الحجاجره	Al-Hajajira
خالو وحيد	Uncle Wahid
خالو وليد	Uncle Walid
خالتو عائدة	Aunt Aida
إيناس	Inas
دمشق	Damascus
لطفي العجمي	Lotfi Al-Ajmi
علي العمقاوي	Ali Al-Amqawi
ابو خليل الخطيب	Abu Khalil Al-Khatib
احمد عزيز ابو الجفرا	Ahmed Aziz Abu Al-Jafra
الحميدية	Al-Hamidiyah
جفرا	Jafra
سليم الغضبان	Salim Al-Ghadban
كندا	Canada
كويكات	Kuwaykat
جباتا الخشب	Jabata Al-Khashab
جدين	Judin
الطيونه	Al-Tayouneh
طيونه") سهيلة")	Suhaila ("Tayouneh")

وندسور	Windsor
خالو رافع (أبو ميار)	Uncle Rafe (Abu Maiar)
ميار	Maiar
الفضل	Al-Fadel
نهاريا	Nahariya
ابو سنان	Abu Snan
كفر ياسيف	Kafr Yasif
جت	Jatt
لبنان	Lebanon
رميش	Rmeish
دير القاسي	Dayr Al-Qassi
عمقا	Amka
السامرة	Al-Samirah
حيفا	Haifa
حسين	Hussein
حسن	Hasan
ابو حسين	Abu Hussein
سليمان زيادة	Suleiman Ziada
قطر	Qatar
قانا	Qana
هولندا	the Netherlands
صور	Tyre
السويد	Sweden
فرنسا	France
امريكا	America
القاسمية	Al-Qasimiyah
البازوريه	Al-Bazouriyeh
استراليا	Australia
برج البراجنة	Bourj el-Barajneh
بيروت	Beirut
خالتو مائسة	Aunt Maesa
مصر	Egypt
موريس	Maurice

خالتو نسرين	Aunt Nisreen
صرعة	Sar'a
عرتوف	Artuf
زكريا	Zakariyya
بيت نتيف	Bayt Nattif
بيت عطاب	Bayt 'Itab
طارق	Tarek
ملاك	Malak
إشوع	Ishwa
عسلين	Islin
بيت أولا	Beit Ula
سعير	Sa'ir
ترشيحا	Tarshiha
ابو محمود الهواري	Abu Mahmoud Al-Hawari
فوزية	Fawzia
كامل	Kamel
فاطمة الهواري	Fatema Al-Hawari
تل عراد	Tel Arad
ركاد الجشي	Rakad Al-Geshi
ابو سامي بشارة	Abu Sami Bishara
اللقيه	Lakiya
احمد	Ahmed
غزة	Gaza
الحاج خليل	Haj Khalil
الشيخ قدورة	Sheikh Qaddoura
قبرص	Cyprus
الشيخ جراح	Sheikh Jarrah
القدس	Jerusalem
علي جروان	Ali Jarwan
عين الأسد	Ein Al-Asad
عيلبون	Eilabun
بيت جن	Beit Jann
مخيم اليرموك	Yarmouk Camp

خالو ظافر	Uncle Zafer
احمد سعيد كروم	Ahmed Said Karroum
الفراضية	Farradiyya
كفر عنان	Kafr ʿInan
لفتا	Lifta
وآخرون	et al.

afterword

Umbilical Discord incorporates testimonies by Palestinian women who have witnessed and survived the ongoing Nakba ("Catastrophe" in Arabic) of 1948. Excerpts of these accounts, retrieved from the Zochrot website, make up the indented, italicized sections of the poems, while the left-justified text embodies a diasporic Palestinian perspective.

Established in 2002, Zochrot is a nonprofit association based in Tel Aviv that seeks "to broaden [within Israeli society] the recognition of the Nakba and the Palestinian refugees' right of return."[1] I scoured the Zochrot website to find every testimony by Palestinian women, and I ended up with a list of around fifty testimonies. The testimonies varied in type (video form with and without accompanying Arabic and/or English transcripts or subtitles; text form in Arabic only, English only, or both Arabic and English; testimonies centered around one person or a group of people from the same area), and they varied in length, with some videos under fifteen minutes and others up to two hours long. I created charts with the Arabic text in the right column and the English translations in the left column, and I began the painstaking translation process. Even for the long testimonies with existing English translations, I noticed that those translations neglected large chunks of the testimonies, and so I had to fill those gaps myself. For the video testimonies, I often strained to understand what the women were saying, either because I could not catch the word(s) they said (i.e., I could not even spell them in Arabic), or because I did not understand the meaning of the words I could sound out in Arabic (where

---

1. Zochrot, https://zochrot.org/en.

searching for the word yielded no results). This latter case happened even with the already available Arabic text. My English translation columns were filled with question-mark placeholders or transliterations for words I could not translate, as in the following example: "We used to get sesame seeds and make (sarabet?) as tall as this house to let it dry, then we'd lay out clothes and spread out the sesame, and we'd fill them in ? and deliver (nwardo) them to Lydd and Ramle." At one point, I made a note in the translation column: "I'm getting emotional, frustrated I can't understand her."

Indeed, I was pushed to ask for help. I tried sitting with my mom so that she could translate the Palestinian Arabic for me—or rather, so that she could explain what the Palestinian women were saying in other Arabic words. After struggling to understand the women herself, my mom told me, "Go ask your uncle Hasan for help." Uncle Hasan, who lives in Syria and speaks fluent English, was graciously able to translate two long testimonies for me, not without me feeling guilty for taxing him with such an arduous task. And, even with his translations, I had to go back, watch the long testimonies, and rephrase the translations. I reached out to an English-speaking cousin of mine, Ghaith, who also translated for me a long Arabic-text testimony. I was so adamant about translating each and every testimony that I even tried to hire a translator, but as my translation document began to exceed 120 pages, I had to admit that I already had more material than I could incorporate into my project.

I think my desire to translate as many of the testimonies as possible stemmed from two fears: the fear of missing out on valuable information from these Palestinian women—an illuminating reflection, a life-changing anecdote, a unique piece of the Palestinian puzzle; and the fear of focusing on my own writing and what I had to say—or what I did not have to say—about my connection to Palestine. I was also caught up in trying to furnish the Palestine growing in my imagination: as I worked through the translations, I felt the need to create a "catalogue" of different elements—long lists of names of people and places, and lists of "food/drink," "land/plants," and "animals." I decided to include, at the end of *Umbilical Discord*, a list of "members"—the names of people and places as they chronologically appear in the collection—to honor the people and lands, to counter the erasure of Palestinian villages by including their original Arabic names, and to indicate the desire I had to build my knowledge of Palestine as a Palestinian who has never set foot in her "homeland."

I eventually began to give poetic form to the testimonial videos and texts, visually interlacing my writing and the stories of various family members with the modified transcriptions and translations, retranslating some of the lines as I went (e.g., I changed "vacationing" to "getting fresh air," which is closer to the freshness of the literal Arabic phrase, "a sniff of air").

While the first two poems in the collection, "dis cord" and "dis location," each focus on a testimony by one woman (Nazmiyya Al-Kilani and Amina Ataba, respectively), the third poem, "dis section," incorporates translations of an Arabic text-only testimonial collection called "The Story of Kuwaykat" ("حكاية الكويكات"), where multiple Palestinians from the Kuwaykat village share their experiences.[2] The fourth poem, "dis ease," is unique in that the left-justified lines are mostly comprised of a different testimonial—my aunt Maesa's account of a dangerous sea voyage from Egypt to Europe with her family

---

2. "Testimony by Nazmiyya al-Kilani," Zochrot, posted February 2021, https://www.zochrot.org/videos/view/56581/en?Testimony_by_Nazmiyya _alKilani_; "Testimony by Amina Ataba," Zochrot, posted March 2022, https://www.zochrot.org/videos/view/56600/en?; and "حكاية الكويكات" (The Story of Kuwaykat), Zochrot, posted September 1, 2008, https://www .zochrot.org/testimonies/view/52293/ar?Kuwaykat_story.

and other Syrian refugees, which I retrieved from her Facebook page and translated from Arabic. The indented and italicized lines in "dis ease" are comprised of translated/poeticized excerpts from the Zochrot testimonials, but unlike the first three poems, here I drew excerpts from multiple testimonies.[3] I also drew from various testimonies for the final poem, "re cord."[4] By the time I was working on these last two poems, I had read through the testimonial material many times, so I gave myself more freedom in incorporating excerpts that I found most startling or that paralleled or juxtaposed with the left-justified column effectively.

I am indebted to the family members and Palestinian elders whose stories shaped this book. I pray this work honors them, and I pray it suggests the breadth and depth of the Palestinian cause—a matter of there and here, of then and now. A matter within reach, in the palms of our hands.

3. Testimonies by Ghosta Dakwar Gharzouzi, Maryam Abdullah Ahmed Shehadeh, Hajja Rukayya al-Sana'a, Nima Hasan Hussein Mubarak Safi, Khadija Safadi, Nazmeiah Muhammad Abdelkader Wahdan, Sarah Abdullah Mahmoud Abu Latifa, Umm Faris al-Sani, and Diya Hussein Muhammad Omar Fa'ur.
4. Testimonies by Ghosta Dakwar Gharzouzi, Nazmeiah Muhammad Abdelkader Wahdan, Khazne Sama'an, Khadija Safadi, Rukayya Abdulsalam Abu Al-Haija, Nima Hasan Hussein Mubarak Safi, Fatema Mansour, Adiba Choucair, and Salwa Naser.